Five Star Amazon Reader Reviews

Horse Listening – The Book: This is an excellent book for beginners and intermediate riders of any discipline. Dressage is about finding balance in ourselves and for our horses. Kathy gives simple, spot-on descriptions of reader direction and then completes them with exercise and a REASON for doing them.

- Barbara Progress

Horse Listening – Book 2: Great read. insightful and easy read that covers almost all areas of training your horse and more. I totally enjoyed it. – Anna Stocking

Horse Listening – Book 3: These books are great! Clear, easy to understand, very helpful for a novice rider like myself. Thank you! - Nae

Five Years of Horse Listening

KATHY FARROKHZAD

With Photographs By

NATALIE BANASZAK

A Collection of Articles from
Horse Listening – The Blog

Published by:

Full Circle Equestrian
P.O. Box 216
Ballinafad, ON, Canada, N0B 1H0

TABLE OF CONTENTS

Introduction

I remember it well, probably because there is so much emotion attached to the first time you press the *publish* button. I had made 14 revisions before that moment. I'd taken a close look at the text, an even closer look for typos. Re-read it again to make sure it really did say what I wanted it to say. Figured out the tags and categories. Thought about what it might feel like to send my words out into the world... not realizing that one day, I would be looking back on five years of writing and riding and thinking and documenting and communicating.

No. I was just worried about what might happen after *publish*.

Would I be ridiculed for my thoughts? Would I even make enough sense to get across what I was thinking? Would it even matter if I could?

I did not have the answers. I did the only thing I felt I could at that juncture. I clicked.

I could actually feel my pulse speed up and I remember my surprise as sweat rolled off my forehead while I was just sitting there! The web page showed it was "working" and next thing I knew, it said the post had been published. Switching to the home page, I reloaded, and sure enough, there was the digitized version of my words!

My worries were (mostly) unfounded and as time went on, I felt more confident in my prose, better able to format the text, lay out the page and endure less overheating.

Now there are five years of writing under my belt. Little did I imagine that at some point, I'd have 358 blog posts on the web site, a regular column in a leading Canadian newspaper, two published articles in equine magazines, an Internet radio interview, and four books with my name on them. What a journey it has been!

More importantly, I met fellow horse lovers from all around the world. Readers shared their horses with me. They told me their stories, shared their knowledge, challenges, and kind words of encouragement. I still marvel at the power of the Internet for making these connections possible.

In celebration of 5 years of blogging, I've reproduced the top 20 blog posts "of all time" (up to this current month) in this one book. If you notice that the chapters count backwards, it's because I've started with the #20 post and worked all the way to the #1 most widely read post in the blog. These have often been shared, reblogged or mentioned over the years. I feel they represent all the facets of what has become *Horse Listening:* from rider's aids, to training tips, to the "why" behind the concepts and to what I feel is most important about horses – their impact on our lives and personal development.

Five years seem like just a blink. And then it also

feels like so much has happened in the meantime. I had no real plans for the blog then, and I'm not sure what is going to happen with it over the next five years. One thing I do know is that this blog has become a part of my *lifestyle* in the same way the horses have. It is more of a way of being rather than just a hobby. I do know that I will keep writing, riding, sharing and listening – because "horse listening" is really what it's all about, for me.

With thanks for reading and being part of the Horse Listening journey.

Kathy

SAFETY FIRST

In all of this book's chapters, as in riding, concern for the horse's well-being, health and longevity is at the forefront of our efforts. It is also the method behind the madness of all the suggestions contained in this book.

As with many physical endeavors, horseback riding requires a certain level of fitness, balance and co-ordination. The unpredictable nature of the horse always adds an element of uncertainty and danger that we needs to be aware of.

Please use any and all of the suggestions in this book at your discretion. Common sense always prevails! Feel free to change anything to meet the needs of you and your horse. Finally, be sure to "listen," because the horse will always let you know if you are on the right track.

20. How To Ride The Stumble Out Of Your Horse

Do you have a horse that seems to regularly trip or stumble, either in the front or hind end?

The footing is good. The path is clear. There were no sudden changes to your direction.

The horse is sound and you know the tack fits well. His feet are trimmed. There are no other underlying physical issues that you are aware of.

Yet your horse stumbles here, trips there, and as time goes on, you learn to just quietly ignore it. After all, the horse is trying his best and there's nothing you can do, right?

WRONG!

If you listen carefully, you might even discover that you are more a part of the equation than you give yourself credit for.

It might be something you are doing. Or it might be something you are NOT doing!

Be an active rider so you can help your horse through these moments. Your strong problem-solving skills are just the ticket to helping your horse develop better balance during riding.

Reasons for Stumbling

The root problem might be one, or a combination of these ideas.

1. Horse is heavy on the forehand.

We know the tell-tale signs for that. The horse is heavy on the bit. The front leg strides are bigger than the hind leg strides. The horse might even feel like he is on a downward slope, leaning in to the ground rather than up away from it.

2. Horse's outline is too long and low.

This might come hand-in-hand with #1. Often, we feel we are being "nice" to let a horse stretch his neck up and/or down, because we are taught that a long rein leads to a softer, lighter contact that is kind. What we aren't always told is that the horse might have to brace his back and tense his muscles to hold a longer body position, especially in order to deal with the weight of a rider in the saddle.

Add to the "strung-out" outline - a hind end that is no longer able to support the weight (because the hind legs have stretched beyond the horse's croup, thereby not allowing for adequate weight carriage) - and there you have it folks - the stumble!

3. Horse speeds up faster and faster in the same gait.

A horse that tends to move his legs faster and faster when you ask for more impulsion or a gait change is a good candidate for a stumble. Again, his weight (and yours) falls forward and the front legs have to carry the majority of the impact.

4. Inadequate engagement.

The opposite can also be true. The horse that "sucks back" is bracing with his front end, effectively pushing backward in the movement or lacking enough energy to maintain balance while progressing forward. This active tension can be a cause for stumbling.

5. Horse needs extra help on one side.

A horse with a weak side (for example, a weak left stifle) could have trouble bringing that hind leg up with the same amount of strength and fluidity as the rest of the body. After the true source of the problem is identified and addressed (i.e. call a veterinarian!), you can support that side with more active riding aimed at building up the muscles around the joint.

6. Horse is overly crooked.

Some horses are particularly stiff to one side. This might be influenced by a natural cause (born that way), or from previous incorrect riding. In either case, much attention needs to be given to at least straightening the horse (even if it is too difficult to get a true bend) while he is moving.

7. You shift your weight to the horse's forehand.

Riders often lean forward in movement. As bipeds, it is what we are naturally programmed to do! However, "listen" carefully to your horse when he stumbles. If he tends to trip when you lean forward, you know the reason why. In this case, you will need to hold your weight back, even if you want to ride in two-point or go over a jump. You *can* hold your weight and change your posture - just be aware!

***

The idea is to re-balance that energy surge to the hind end rather than let it run out the front end. Think half-halts, and use them as often as necessary to help your horse maintain balance. Constantly work on that re-balance - you may need to do the whole thing three, four, five times in a row, in *rhythm with the horse's strides*, to help the horse understand he needs to sift his weight backward. This might be very difficult for a horse that is not used to working from the hind end.

.   But it is essential, first, to prevent the stumble, and second, to keep the horse sound long-term.

Good luck!

---

4 Steps to Prevent Stumbling

1. Leg on for impulsion. Even the fast-footed horse is disengaged and needs to bring his hind end underneath him. So put your legs on and be ready for more movement!

2. Commit your body to the energy surge. The horse *should* lurch forward a bit. This is good. Go with him. Be sure you don't stop the forward inclination by pulling back on the reins.

3. Straighten the horse (if needed). Use the energy surge to straighten the horse, left or right as needed. Just guide the energy into straightness, don't stifle it.

4. Half-halt. This is key. Without the half-halt immediately after the energy surge, you tell the horse to run away. You don't want your horse to flee your aids, so within a moment after your legs and straightness, your half-halt should come on (brace your seat, back, arms momentarily).

Then release.

19. How Do You Know Your Horse Is Using His Back?

Let's face it: we see many people riding their horses with sunken backs, disengaged hind ends, and heavy footfalls. If *they* do it, why shouldn't we? Are we being conceited, ostentatious, pompous or pretentious?

Are we simply just *too picky*?

No, it's none of the above.

It's because we care.

Enough.

To put in the work.

Because it's a fact: learning to feel the back of the horse, especially in movement, is not for the weak-hearted.

It requires hours of dedicated practice, oodles of lesson dollars, numerous requests for forgiveness from the horse, and perhaps most difficult of all, countless adjustments to our internal neural pathways, both physical and mental.

Is all this worth it?

OF COURSE IT IS!

In the long run, our primary motivation for self-improvement in riding is for the sake of the horse's health. We want horses that live well, staying strong and vigorous long into their old age. And a horse that uses his back is carrying the rider's weight to his best advantage.

Feel it.

The round back feels loose, bouncy, rolling, supple. It feels like the horse is having an easy time carrying your weight. He is less on his front legs and more on the haunches.

He gives you the impression that he can stop on a dime or turn on a thought. He is forward, active and content. The energy from the hind end easily flows through the shoulders and you notice larger, longer strides, and bouncier, more active gaits.

If you have trouble loosening enough to sit the trot, (you might be shocked to discover that) you might have even MORE trouble riding the trot of a horse that is using his back. This is because the horse's natural gaits become amplified when the back moves freely and it might be more difficult for you to stay with the loftier movement. You'd be better off posting so that you can encourage your horse to keep his soft, active back.

The same is true with the canter - the strides are more exaggerated and you feel more swing in the ride. Be prepared to let your lower back flow with the activity - anything less and you'll be stifling the horse's enthusiastic offering.

Basically, if you feel the gaits getting bigger, rounder, bouncier and maybe a bit harder to ride, then you know you are on the right track!

The Tight Back...

... feels just that - tight.

... restricts the movement of the legs.

... creates short, choppy strides that lurch and jerk.

... prevents establishment of a good forward-flowing rhythm.

... causes the horse to move on the forehand, taking the brunt of the concussion on the front legs.

... can be the culprit behind sore backs and "mystery" lamenesses.

The irony is that the horse can appear to be more "comfortable" to ride, in that the movement is smaller and shorter and thus easier for most riders to follow. If you think your horse feels smooth and comfortable, consider whether or not the smooth feeling is caused by the horse locking his back and preventing movement.

Your first clue will be in the size of the stride - if it is a short stride, particularly in the hind legs, then the horse in NOT using his back.

One last secret: The horse's back is often a reflection of the rider's back. If the rider is tight and short in her movement, the horse can't help it but stay tight and short.

It might take many months of finding the "feel" in your back and then learning to maintain th required movement just to allow your horse's back the freedom to swing and let the energy through.

18 On Slobber, Snorts and Sheath Sounds: 3 Ways to Your Horse's Back

Everywhere you look, people are missing out on three significant "happy horse" signs. I'm not talking about the perky-eared cute faces looking for treats, or the mutual grooming kind of affection horses share with each other. This time, I'm talking about signs you can see while the horse is being ridden.

It is a fact - horses who move well and freely have a better time during the ride. They learn to look forward to their time in the saddle, and they even improve physically and mentally.

Although we often talk about the hind legs being the "engine" of good movement, it is the back of the horse that is the key to all things great in riding. Think about it - picture the horse with the swaying, supple back and you will almost always recognize the beauty and harmony depicted in the horse's overall way of going. It doesn't matter the discipline - a good back means good movement and long-term health of the horse.

Read on to find out all about slobber, snorts and sheath sounds, and how they relate to the horse's back.

Slobber

Why do some horses have a white lipstick when they're being ridden?

Some people say that slobber happens when a horse has his neck so short and the reins are so tight that he can't swallow. They argue that the horse would be able to prevent drooling if only he could open and close his mouth. Maybe his head and neck is positioned in a way that he can't swallow. Or the problem is the bit that is in his mouth; the piece of metal makes the horse unable to close the lips and swallow.

The reasons go on and on.

But surely you have seen a (maybe nervous or tense) horse ridden with no contact and/or bit, yet still with a dry mouth for an entire ride.

And quite possibly, you've seen the exact opposite: a horse lunged with no side reins or any contact whatsoever, carrying his head any which way he pleases, developing a line of foam in the corner of the mouth and around the lips.

What of the western horse being ridden in a snaffle bit (or any variation of bitless bridles) with very infrequent contact, dripping drool like the highest level dressage horse?

It's All About the Back

I've seen and ridden these horses and experienced their variations of slobber. And I've come to one conclusion: that slobber is connected not so much to the mouth, jaw or swallowing - but to the back of the horse. Develop movement from the hind end, get a nice rhythm and back swing, and presto: discover the path to slobber.

If you think about it, the root to all good in riding rests in the back. If you can encourage an elastic, round, swinging back, you know your horse is on his way to riding pleasure. Not only does he benefit from the work, chances are, he might actually be enjoying it.

However, don't stop there. It's not only the horse's back you have to consider - think about *your* back too. Because your back can be holding your horse's back back (did you follow that?), which results in tension all around. If your back is resistant or unmoving, the same will happen to your horse. He won't be able to carry your weight effectively, nor will he be able to let the energy flow through his topline. So freeing your back up and developing more mobility will also lead your horse to lipstick slobber.

Snorts

Happy horse sign number two is the snort.

Physically, the snorts happen when the horse takes a deeper breath. He might reach farther underneath the body, work straighter and therefore more through the abs or put in a sudden moment of effort. For whatever reason, he then has to take a deeper breath and then he lets it all out in a body-shaking snort. Sometimes, the snort is accompanied by a neck arching or reaching forward that might catch you off guard if you're not expecting it.

In any case, the snort is a releasing/ relaxing/ letting go of tension and yes, you might notice the horse's eye soften or his gait become more buoyant. Watch a little longer and you might see him settle in his work, find his rhythm or soften in the mouth. You might also see some accompanying slobber!

Sheath Sounds

Now this one is the clincher. Of course, if you ride a mare, you miss out on the most obvious, tell-tale sign of a tight back. In geldings, the tight back causes a tight sheath area, which then results in air movement - that sound you hear EVERY stride the horse takes.

People often say that the sound is caused by a dirty sheath area. But if you own or care for a gelding regularly, chances are that you can honestly say that the sheath has been cleaned and yet the sound continues. So what gives?

Yes, folks, it's all about the back yet again.

Try this: when you hear the sound, go for a 3-5 stride canter from the trot. Then trot again. Make sure you half-halt the trot as you come out of the canter, so that the horse doesn't just trot faster faster *faster*. Rather, you want to use the canter to add more impulsion to the trot. Feel for more bounce, more air time between strides. See if you can get a snort.

And then listen for the sheath sound. Maybe it stops for a few strides. Maybe it isn't quite as loud. Or maybe it goes away altogether. If you "listen" carefully enough, you will begin to recognize a pattern to what causes the sound.

Maybe you can make it go away for only a couple of strides. Pay attention to what caused the sound to go away. Then try to duplicate it. Maybe your horse is too tense for the sound to ever go away. But give it a good try, every ride. Eventually, you might be able to make it go away just using your riding skills. And you'll know that your horse is using his back in a healthier manner.

*****

So there you have it: three sure-fire ways of knowing if your horse is actually loose in his back!

17. 7 Essential Aids For An Epic Canter Transition

When you first learn to canter, it's about all you can do to get the horse to change his legs from a two-beat trot to a three-beat canter. You do pretty much anything you can to make the transition happen - lean forward, kick, kick harder, kick some more, let the reins go, use your voice....

You might feel like the canter is a huge speed-up from the trot, and when the horse finally does canter, the euphoric feeling of strength and power sends you into a rocking horse motion that just can't really be adequately described to the non-rider.

But then you get better at it.

You realize that the canter departure doesn't have to resemble a rocket launch. You develop your aids till both you and your horse look a lot more civilized - and a lot less frantic. At some point, you realize that you can trot, maintain the trot rhythm, and elegantly step into the canter. Your aids become invisible, prompting less educated onlookers to think that the horse is reading your mind.

So how exactly do you develop an epic canter transition? How do the aids become refined enough to create a smooth, balanced and active upward transition? In the following seven steps, I've tried to break down each component of the transition in order to explain the nuances that go into a split-second movement! Although it might seem a little complicated, I hope that it can describe each moment that goes into a better developed canter departure.

Once you know each part that goes into the one movement, you might be able to problem-solve your departures with your horse and focus on one or two aspects as needed.

1. It All Starts With the Seat

Well, we already know this. But how does the seat exactly play into the transition? First off, your seat should be trotting when the horse is trotting. So if you are sitting the trot, your seat bones are actually moving in the rhythm of the trot. Be sure to promote a strong but not fast rhythm - one that your horse finds easy to move in while remaining supple.

If you are posting the trot, sit the last few strides before the canter. Use your seat to draw up the horse's hind legs, asking for more impulsion.

2. Use the Inside Leg/Outside Rein

The inside leg has a very important job in this moment. Apply the whole leg (from ankle up) at the girth to ask the horse for a mild bend to prepare for the inside lead. If your horse has a tendency to lean in just before the transition, your inside leg becomes even more critical in helping the horse maintain balance by not allowing him to drop his rib cage toward the middle of the ring.

The outside rein does little except to act as a "neck rein" - the one that sits onto the horse's neck and prevents him from drifting to the outside. It also can apply the half-halt aids before and after the departure.

3. Half-Halt Preparation

Do one or two or three half-halts *before* the transition.

We often tend to "throw everything away" (as in, lengthen the reins, take the legs off the horse, fall to the horse's front) as we head into the gait change. Fight that impulse and instead, keep the horse together. Keep your*self* together!

Falling to the forehand and trotting faster before the canter almost always ensures a low-quality canter gait. Although the horse might transition, he will likely be on the forehand, braced in his neck and jaw and hollow in his back. He will also likely fall back to the trot sooner than later, no matter what you do to keep him going, because he simply can't maintain his balance with that posture.

Instead, after you ask for impulsion, half-halt the horse to balance his weight to the hind end. Keep your legs on for impulsion after the half-halt.

4. Use the Outside Leg - Ask For the Lead

The outside leg initiates the lead. Some people call it a "windshield wiper" motion: swing your lower leg behind the girth to ask for the first stride. The horse's outside hind leg should strike off into the lead as your leg reaches back.

5. Canter With Your Seat

So far, your seat should have been trotting. Now, it needs to transition. You go from two seat bones moving in tandem with the horse in the trot, to a canter motion with the inside seat bone leading (to allow for the horse to take the inside lead). Your seat now needs to promote the canter movement – swinging back and forth thanks to your supple lower back.

Keep your shoulders fairly still by moving *through* your back. The swinging movement allows for the *illusion* of your shoulders staying still while the horse is moving.

6. Use the Half-Halt Again

Just because the horse is now in canter doesn't mean that you should stop riding! Many of us tend to freeze in our aids, opting instead to just hang on to the increased movement of the canter. Well, as soon as you have enough balance and are able, ride actively again.

Half-halt - once, twice, three times maybe - in the rhythm of the canter. This helps the horse to stay "together" after the transition. The sudden surge of energy needs to be controlled so that it doesn't just fall on the horse's shoulders and forehand.

7. Canter on!

Now all you have to do is commit to the horse's movement. Your seat should allow the movement that your horse offers, and it's your job to not let your upper body fall forward/backward/sideways while your seat follows, follows and follows (unless you do another half-halt).

* * *

When you first start paying attention to each of these aspects of the canter transition, you might need to actually think through every part, talking your body into the necessary activity while negotiating the canter movement. But rest assured - with practice and time, things become more and more automatic, and then you can focus more on your horse's specific needs.

Though we are talking about so many steps all subdivided here, in reality, it all comes together within a few seconds - from preparation, to the request, strike-off and follow-through. Eventually, it happens so seamlessly that the departure becomes just a quick thought - one that transpires between both you and your horse in an epic, seemingly mind-reading fashion!

16. 6 Ways to Unleash the Power of Your Riding Seat

First, there are hands and legs. When we learn to ride, we tend to guide the horse primarily through the use of our hands, then through our legs. Rein aids and leg aids reign supreme (pun intended!): left rein here, right rein there, inside leg, outside leg... you know the routine.

Without a doubt, it is essential to learn the use of hands and legs to achieve a basic sense of control of the horse - it is not always a pleasant experience to have a spirited equine expressing his enthusiasm while you hang on for dear life!

As you become more subtle in the aiding process, you will begin to discover just how powerful the seat can be.

As time goes on, however, you begin to develop a sense for the horse's balance, for the energy that moves through the body, and for the 'release' that the horse can achieve given the opportunity. You begin to develop 'feel' through your seat.

When is the horse lifting/dropping his back? When are the hind legs underneath the body? How much energy is needed to allow just enough 'forward' for the horse to reach but not so much that he will fall to the forehand? As you become more subtle in the aiding process, you will begin to discover just how powerful the seat can be in guiding the horse without disturbing and interfering in his movement.

1. Find Your Seat.

Get yourself a good instructor that knows how to *teach* the finer points of using the seat during riding. There are a lot of people who use their seat effectively but for one reason or another, cannot seem to be able to explain well enough to break it down into achievable skills. You must learn how to activate your seat bones, and differentiate between using the seat versus weight aids.

Getting control of the "inner" components of the seat will take time and perseverance as this is likely not a typical movement that you're used to. Look at it as a 2-year goal - one that takes thousands of repetitions to master. Lunging on a reliable, rhythmical school horse might be on the menu in order to allow you to free your lower back, hips and thighs enough to begin to feel the physical requirements of using your seat.

Know that it is extremely worthwhile to put that much effort into the skill acquisition, as everything, including your balance, revolves around an effective use of the seat.

2. Develop Effective Half-halts.

The seat is a key component to a half-halt. Without the seat, your half-halt is about as effective as a pull from your hand, or a kick from the leg. Neither aids really help the horse in rebalancing, which is the ideal result desired from the half-halt. Use your seat to keep your horse "with" you - brace your lower back to rebalance the horse's momentum and weight to the hind end.

Use your seat bones laterally to allow half-halts to effect one side only (horse leaning on one side, or drifting through a shoulder) and alternately, use diagonal half-halts (inside seat bone to outside supporting rein) to encourage better use of the hind end by the horse.

3. Free Your Seat to Free the Horse's Back.

Encourage your horse to move 'forward' - rather than use your legs to kick a horse onward, use your seat to encourage the more balanced sense of being 'forward'. In the trot, you can follow along with the horse in a more giving way through your entire seat, opening on the "up" phase of the posting trot (without actually posting). Your seat has the power to encourage the horse to "step through" with his hind legs and develop a lovely rhythmical swinging of the back that will allow for a willing and supple response to your aids.

4. Transition From the Seat.

Rather than using your hands for a downward

transition, or your legs for an upward transition, use your seat as the "root" to the transition - either upward *or* downward. Move your seat into the next gait (even if it is a downward transition) and expect the horse to respond almost entirely off your seat aid. Use hands/legs only if absolutely necessary, *after* you applied the seat aid.

5. Change Directions.

Did you know that you can allow a horse to turn smoothly and in balance simply from a seat aid? Your hands work on keeping the horse *straight* through the turn, and your seat works from the waist down to turn the horse from his middle. Soon you will be free from "steering" the horse with your hands. Eventually, the horse will appear to read your mind because the aids will become incredibly subtle and shared only between you and your horse. The only visible result will be the *lack* of fuss and a total unison in movement.

6. Stop! (No Hands Needed!)

After a series of half-halts, it will only take your seat to stop the horse's legs. Simply stop moving and "halt" with your seat. Remember to keep your legs on as the horse still needs to complete the halt by bringing his legs underneath him. Your thought process could go like this: "bring your (hind) legs under, bring your legs under, bring your legs under, halt." It will work every time, give it a try!

The above ideas are just the beginning. Use your seat to do lateral work, half-passes, flying changes and even pirouettes. The more you learn about and activate your seat, the more you will discover about the incredible power of the seat.

15. 20 Ways Horse Riding Becomes Life Itself

At first, horse riding is just like any other skill you want to learn. You put effort in and eventually become more effective as time goes on.

At some point, things begin to change. Somehow, without you necessarily knowing about it, the seemingly sport specific skills the horses have taught you take on more meaning. "Horsey" skills become relevant in your daily activities, even when the circumstances have nothing at all to do with horses.

While we develop as riders, we also grow as human beings. Not only do we grow in terms of physical ability, but perhaps even more so, we grow in character.

Situations that used to affect us one way no longer bother us in the same manner, not because the circumstances themselves are any different, but more due to how we have learned to deal with them.

Then we realize that the true teachers are the horses themselves. All we have to do is learn to listen.

Horse riding becomes life when...

1. The patience you develop working with your horse becomes the patience you use with your friends and colleagues.

2. The body language you use to communicate with the horses becomes your source of confidence in group activities.

3. The coordination you learn on the back of the horse keeps you safe from unexpected physical mishaps.

4. Heavy lifting/pulling/pushing/hoof cleaning develops your strength enough to allow you to fluidly function during physically taxing circumstances.

5. Facing your fears while on another's four legs teaches you how to have courage in the face of life's

many difficulties.

6. You learn to temper your (often over-scheduled) daily routines by slowing down to meet the simplicity of horse life.

7. The leadership skills your horse teaches you carries into your work and relationship interactions.

8. The self-confidence you develop from knowing you can influence a powerful animal seeps into every interaction you have with people.

9. You learn from horses that it's okay for things to get worse, because after things get worse, they always get better.

10. You discover that taking shortcuts might not be to your benefit in the long run; some things have to take the time they need to take.

11. When certain maneuvers get a little difficult (like riding through a corner), all you need is a little extra impulsion to smooth things out.

12. Sometimes, you just have to let go (especially when the horse bucks and bucks)!

13. In general, riding (life) isn't about brute strength - it's about subtle technique and strategy.

14. There is no such thing as a day off - you begin to value the rewards that hard work reaps.

15. The work has to get done whether you feel up to it or not – invariably, you learn to prioritize responsibilities and get it all done.

16. You understand completely how asking nicely is always better than demanding.

17. There is no such thing as instant gratification. There is only hard work and step-by-step development.

18. You seek perfection, but realize that you can rarely reach it!

19. The path is more important than the end result.

20. Although we all have our own "conformation faults" that might work against us, we can overcome almost anything with skill, time and effort.

14. The #1 Rider Problem: Pulling to Frame a Horse

Each year, I try to pinpoint one essential rider problem that is prevalent with most riders. Two years ago, we discussed the outside rein, last year it was the leg aid and so this year, let's discuss something we all do or have probably done at one point in our riding career.

Admit it! You've probably tried it yourself.

Pull.

Any direction will do, really. Up, down, open rein, closed rein, back to the thigh... we can get creative about it. The main goal is to get that horse to finally give, usually through the jaw, poll and maybe neck area, so that there can be less tension, or pull, or tightness through the head, neck and back. The horse also might level out into a frame that is desirable in your riding discipline.

Most horses do "let go" at some point and emulate softness. The only problem is that while the front end can contort enough to find the release from you, the middle and hind end cannot lie. The back drops or sags, the hind legs shorten stride, the hind end might even "camp out" - essentially, the horse travels with a longer back than he might otherwise, precisely because through the act of pulling, we have blocked the energy that is travelling to the front of the horse.

But we do it anyway. (Trust me - I have the T-shirt.)

****

"Framing" a horse is one of those essential things we tend to obsess over once we can keep our balance well enough to be able to work on other things. By then, we can "feel" well enough to know that the horse is moving stiffly and with uneven steps. We can feel the tension radiate through the horse from the jaw to the back and into our very core.

Once in a while, the horse loosens up and we discover this tension-free, bouncy-floaty feeling that we know is right, but then, as soon as we turn to look the other way, the horse falls out of that riding heaven. We are left forever after wanting to emulate that feeling in every ride.

So we pull.

But there is another way.

In order to truly "round" a horse - versus "frame" a horse - you want the energy to come over the top line. You want to feel the forward thrust of the hind legs that seems to bolster movement rather than stifle it. You want to let that energy come "through" rather than stop it.

But you can't exactly let it all go either.

Aye, there's the eternal rub.

Regardless of your rein length, and your riding

discipline, you can't "drop the connection" if you want to contain energy. Well, unless both you and your horse are at a level of self-carriage that allows you to control your balance with nothing but seat, leg and weight aids.

Let's assume most of us are not at that level.

1. Half-Halt

Start with a half-halt. Use it to prepare your horse for the upcoming "go" aid.

After you half-halt, give just a little. The idea isn't to pull. It's just a chance for you to create a better connection before you send the horse forward. Create the space but don't completely drop the horse.

2. Then Go

This is the critical part.

Instead of pulling back and reducing energy, you need to build up controlled energy. You need to bolster, encourage, *engage*.

Then, you need to ask your horse to do the same.

You might use just a seat aid. Or you might combine both the seat and the leg. Whatever you decide to do, the result should be that your horse steps deeper with the hind legs and responds with a surge of energy that might even give you a small whip-lash effect. Be ready for it and go with the horse.

3. How to Round

If you just let everything go, and the horse did in

fact energize, then he will either just run faster-faster in the gait, or fall to the forehand or both. Think of a tube of toothpaste as the toothpaste squirts out of the front end.

So to control that energy, and to transfer it over the topline of the horse and encourage the horse to round, you have to do something that will "catch" that energy and recycle it to stay within the horse. This is where a second effective half-halt becomes critical.

At the right moment, you have to say "no" to the go. But it must occur after the initial give and go part.

If your timing is right, you might feel your horse grow underneath you. You might feel him lift up like you imagine an airplane lifts - front end high, hind end low.

You will certainly feel the energy surge and a power you might not be used to.

If you're lucky, you might get a snort from your horse. Then you know you are on the right track for sure!

Finally, you might be surprised to discover that your horse naturally rounds when all the requirements are brought together. Suddenly, and apparently from nowhere, he might soften the jaw, thicken through the neck, round his back (and you will feel like you're floating along on a trampoline-like movement) and step deeper underneath with his hind legs.

And this will happen all at once!

4. Maintain

This last part is something we don't often think about. Once we get "it", we assume that the horse will just stay that way because he loves us so much!

But alas, we discover quickly that if we can't maintain the status quo, the horse's level of ability will quickly diminish to the base level of our riding skills.

To keep the roundness, you have to keep riding forward - with the half-halt, the go and then the no - in a cycle, round and round, over and over.

Then, and only then, will you have true "roundness" and a horse that moves happily, with strength, in a way that will help to keep him sound for years and years

How To Round A Horse (Versus Frame)

1. Half-halt to prepare

2. "Go" to engage

3. Second half-halt to round (energy over the top line)

4. Repeat to maintain roundness

*There is no pull in this process, just an unchanging rein length that works well for your horse at his level of training.

13. Top 10 Ways to Be A Star (Horse Riding) Student

You've booked your lesson.

You've paid your money (or will right after the lesson).

You're taking the time and you've spent effort getting your horse ready.

So now you *think* you're ready for the lesson. But think again.

Being a star student in horseback riding is an art to itself. Aside from the many variables (like the weather, distractions, mood of your horse) that might play into your lesson, there are many other factors that are critical to making the ride enjoyable and useful for you, your horse, and yes, even your instructor!

There is no greater pleasure than the one AFTER your lesson, when you can bask in the glow of hard-earned sweat, and reflect longingly on all the feels, aids and balances that you will try to emulate without your instructor's presence over the next week.

In the meantime, take a look-see through this Top-10 list to see how you rate in your Star search!

P.S. This items on this list assume that you have your own horse and are riding independently, although many could also apply to a riding school situation.

10. Do Your Homework.

In other words, don't wait until the lesson to finally pull your horse out of the back field. If you know your horse always goes better the day after you ride, ride him the day *before* your lesson, so he is at his best when your instructor arrives. If you need to give your horse a day off, then ride two days before and let him rest in between. If you haven't worked in a ring for the past month, book your lesson for a day three weeks down the line, after you've had many rides on your own to get him even slightly "legged up."

9. Be On Time.

If you set the lesson for 10am, be groomed, tacked, bridled, helmet on and maybe even in the ring (depending on your instructor's preference) by 10. Don't make her stand around to watch you groom, unless that is part of the lesson. Try to max out your time with her, preferably in the ring!

8. Be Warmed Up.

You don't have to run your horse off his feet, but it would be very helpful to have him working with you by the time your instructor arrives. Even if your lesson ends up going a bit shorter, the warmed-up horse will be ready to go (as will you) and again, you can get the most value for your time. If you know your horse takes 20 minutes to just begin to loosen up, do that before your lesson.

7. Park Your Ego at the Gate.

This one can be tough. We all have insecurities and fear factors that are difficult to let go of in the face of even constructive criticism. Letting go of your ego must be learned just as any riding skill you attempt. Try, try again, and do your best to not let your feelings interfere with your ride. Let your instructor do and say what she thinks will benefit you the most. Otherwise, you'll get lots of sugar coating and no results.

6. Think Later.

I guarantee that most of us think too much while we are riding. Although thinking seems to be necessary when you are reprogramming your body to do new things, it is a hindrance when we are trying to move in tandem with a horse. Things happen too quickly for you to have the time to think, send messages back and forth through your body, and then hope for a good result.

So think as little as possible and do as much as possible. Save your thinking and questions for when you are on the ground, before or after the lesson. In the meantime, put every ounce of your energy into focusing on your aids and your horse.

5. Don't Stop Riding.

This happens all the time and seems counter-intuitive to learning. As soon as we are challenged with a new concept, we stop the horse, drop the reins, sit flat and begin to consider. Which is exactly what the horse doesn't need. Imagine that your instructor is telling you something that is relevant for that *second*. And if you don't ride it out, you miss the opportunity to learn.

Not only that, once you stop, your horse thinks he's gone on vacation (and so does your body) and you lose all the tone and balance you worked so hard to achieve.

So - keep riding, even if you are grappling with a thought (see #6) and don't really know what to do.

4. Respond Quickly.

Many riders go round and round and round, seemingly oblivious to their instructor's suggestions. So, for example, your instructor sees a good opportunity for you to get your horse into a balanced canter, out of the trot, in just that particular corner, in that particular time frame (which is usually only seconds). She tells you to canter. And you don't. But you trot on, past the corner, past the next corner, and then, finally, step into your first canter stride on the straight line.

Although you did get the canter, your horse is now on his forehand, strung out and struggling to take that first stride from the hind end. The straight line was not a help to your horse, which was exactly why your instructor asked for it in the corner.

Let's say your instructor didn't give you enough time to prepare for the corner. Maybe her instructions were a little later than you needed them to be. What then?

Canter as soon as possible after the moment. Or, make a sharp turn, head right back to the set-up area, and attempt the corner again. No need to worry, just do it.

3. Listen, Try and Trust.

These three qualities may take a long time to develop if you don't do them intuitively on your own. But let's face it - you are asking someone to teach you what they know. So of course, it's important to listen to what they say, even if you don't agree at the moment. Then, give it a try. Trust that they are here to get the best out of you, and have your best interests in mind. If you get to a point that you cannot do these three things, maybe it's time to find another instructor.

2. Make A Change.

The best students have enough skill and gumption (is that a word?) to make a difference in their horse, *based on what their instructor is saying.* So if she wants you to get your horse to use his hind end, then do it. If you think you already did it, but your horse doesn't respond, do it again! Or do something else. Or pop in a half-halt and then use your seat and leg again. In any case, make something happen. It might not be the right change, but do something. Then you can fine-tune the horse's response.

1. Stop Talking and RIDE!

Hands up if you are one of those riders that talks while they ride! When your instructor is in the ring, don't! Instead, listen, try, do, do again, change something... focus all your energy on your own body and the horse. Then talk about it after the ride or through the walk breaks.   Trust me, this list is based on personal experience!

Although I've taken lessons for more years than I can count, I have to admit that each of these points take time to actually learn to do well. But every one of them is worth the effort, and makes your lesson experience more positive, more educational, and most importantly, more beneficial for your horse.

Because he is the one that matters the most!

12. Two Upper Body Secrets To Riding Success

Sometimes it is better to focus on just one or two skills than to try to fix everything all the time.

We've previously considered the importance of the riding seat in all things horseback. The seat is the source of all strength, balance and looseness. Without the seat, all other aids become postures at best and completely unusable at worst. So before all else, put your effort into your seat.

However, as your seat develops, and improvement in balance allows you to become more aware of your arms, legs, torso and weight, you can begin to put more emphasis on other areas of your body.

In typical riding lessons, we often break down positional faults into bits and pieces - inside leg/outside seat bone/outside rein/watch your head tilt/dropped shoulder/collapsed hip - and the list goes on and on. It is true that as riders, we need to become as body aware as athletes in other sports that require balance and positional outlines (such as ballet, gymnastics, skating or dancing).

But instead of critiquing each movement into a multitude of positional corrections, it is possible to simplify things to get the best out of your body, in a way that is easy to remember and perhaps even easy(-ish) to do.

The key to an effective riding position is to move your body as one whole, to send just one cohesive signal to the horse. So let's focus on the body as a whole unit.

There are two essential upper-body skills to learn so that you can maintain an ideal balance and support your horse in his movements to the best of your ability.

1) Position Your Core To the Direction You Want To Go

Think of your belly button area as your core. If you are going straight, your core should be straight. It should also be in line with your horse's shoulders. If your horse isn't straight underneath you, you might need to correct his position with a shoulder-fore, a straighter use of the outside rein, or some other aid that will allow your horse to align his body.

When you go to turn, open your core into the turn. We often tend to point our shoulders too far to the outside, or too far to the inside, depending on the straightness of our bodies. Know your own tendency and work to counter it.

If you know you tend to point your core to the left (regardless of direction of travel), be prepared to put in the extra work to open to the right. You might also have to reduce the "openness" when travelling left, because that direction is likely easier for you to turn into. Try not to over-turn in that direction.

Now the key: keep your head, shoulders, elbows *and hands* aligned with your body (the hands should not have a mind of their own). Instead of letting each body part do something on their own, keep them working in coordination with each other. Become "one".

What to Avoid

Try to keep your shoulders level while you open into the turn; don't tilt into the turn like a motorcycle

Try to stay "tall"; many people have a tendency to collapse through the hip area, thereby dropping their inside shoulder as they negotiate the turn

2) Loosen Through the Lower Back

The second most important skill is to be able to

loosen your lower back at will. Riders often resist the movements of their horses in their lower backs. When your back moves less than needed, you might be restricting the horse's movements without even knowing it. The bigger your horse moves, the more your lower back needs to be able to give.

As your horse moves, your lower back loosens (momentarily in stride) to allow your lower abs to come through to the front of the saddle. This happens in both the trot and canter, although there is more movement when cantering.

If you can move with your horse, you might notice that your horse takes more confident, forward-moving strides. As you develop your strength, you can even dictate stride rhythm through the movement of your seat and lower back, alternating resistance with following.

***

By focusing on just these two aspects of riding, you should be able to fix many other smaller positional problems that depend on a supple, correctly held upper body. Remember that by keeping all the "pieces" together, you can become much clearer and more balanced to the horse.

11. Stop Kicking The Horse!

    Too often, riders are determined to make their horses go with a swift kick or two (or three). At best, the horse lurches forward with arched back and raised neck, scrambling to get his legs underneath him despite being thrown to the forehand. At worst, the horse becomes resentful of the leg aid and learns to resist or even demonstrate his discomfort by kicking out, rearing or bucking.

Did you know that leg aids are used for more than just "go"? Leg aids are such an integral part of your ride that you simply can't do without them!

As you become a better rider, you will discover that the legs have so many messages to communicate other than "go".

Talk to different riders and they'll tell you the various uses of leg aids. Here are a few examples:

1. Impulsion

The most important result coming from your leg aids is impulsion. Ideally, the lightest lower leg squeeze should communicate an increase in movement from your horse. Two legs squeezing at the same time ask for a "scoot forward", causing the horse to tuck his hind under and release a surge of energy forward. Physiologically, the horse's hind legs should step deeper underneath the body and allow the horse to begin the process of carrying more weight in the hind end.

2. Stride Length

Ideally, a deeper reach should mean a rounder back and an increase in stride length. Paired with half-halts, the energy obtained can be redirected in many ways - to a longitudinal stretch over the back, to a higher head and neck elevation and/or to more animated action through the entire body.

One leg can be used to create a deeper hind leg stride on that side of the horse. Theoretically, you could influence just one hind leg with the corresponding leg aid.

3. Bend

Use of one leg aid should encourage your horse to move away from that pressure. True bend (i.e. not a neck bend) should always begin at the seat, be reinforced by the leg, and then be contained with the reins.

4. Hind end position

Using your leg behind the girth should indicate that the hind end steps away from that pressure. Use of your outside leg behind the girth encourages the horse to move into a haunches in ("travers") position. Using your inside leg behind the girth is the key to the renvers (counter-bend), when the horse bends to the outside of the direction of movement.

5. Keep Moving

Two legs used at the same time could mean "keep doing what you were doing". This understanding is essential for movement such as the back-up, where the reins should be the last factor in the movement, and the legs (and seat) the first.

Ideally, the horse should continue backing up *without* increased rein pressure until your legs soften and your seat asks for a halt.

6. Lift the Back

A gentle heel or spur lifting action underneath the rib cage should encourage the horse to lift his back. Of course, this aid is used in conjunction with the seat and hands but the legs can be an effective motivator for the horse to lift his rib cage and "round" in the movement.

7. Lateral Movement

The positioning of your inside leg at the girth and outside leg behind the girth should combine to indicate a lateral movement. Where your seat goes and how your hands finish the movement will differentiate the shoulder-fore from the shoulder-in from the leg yield from the half-pass.

With the exception of the leg yield, your legs position in a way that encourages inside bend and catch the outside hind end (from swinging out). Finally, the horse will proceed to step in the direction of movement if that is required.

Give Up On Kicking!

Kicking your horse only stuns, disturbs, imbalances, and hurts. Although kicking might be a useful way to start out for a beginning rider, once you have better balance in your seat and a more consistent contact with the bit, aim toward using your legs with more purpose.

Learn how to use your legs in the rhythm of the movement. Working against the movement only serves to irritate the horse because he simply cannot respond if the timing is out of sync with the footfalls. Good, effective leg aids work within the movement and are generally not noticeable. Great legs look like they are doing nothing at all.

In all cases, the essential thing you need to do is to keep soft, loose legs draped gently on your horse's side. In this manner, the legs are kind, responsive, clear and secure. The horse knows he can rely on the communication he is receiving from the leg aids, and with repetition, will know just what to do when!

10. Top 10 Ways To Reward Your Horse

As riders, we need to look for any excuse to celebrate our horse's achievements. Good riders are forever thankful for their equine's efforts as they push further stronger deeper and reach new heights. A happy horse is a willing partner, and many horses will give everything they have if they feel your acknowledgement and generosity of spirit.

Don't fool yourself.

Your horse knows exactly how you're feeling during the ride. They can "mind read" (more like body read) and know precisely when you are frustrated, upset, angry and conversely, when you are relaxed, forgiving, joyful and ecstatic. We all know that positive reinforcement is as powerful a way to communicate as any other, and likely more appreciated by your four-legged friend.

Rewarding your horse doesn't have to be done on the ground with a treat in hand. In fact, encouragement received under saddle is more immediate and fulfilling than anything that is done on the ground after you ride. The key is to identify the right time to communicate your approval, and to know how to do it *in movement*.

Without further discourse, here are ten simple ways to let your horse know he is on the right track.

10. **Think,   "Yay/Wow/Great/Fantastic"** or whatever you feel at that moment, and be convinced that your horse can read your mind. Even though horses *can't* read minds, they can definitely read the involuntary messages your body sends through your seat, legs and hands - and they know if the thought was positive or negative. So yes, just *thinking* something nice will transfer seamlessly into your horse's mind.

9. **Say a soft, low "good" under your breath** so only he can hear it. You don't have to share your thank-you with the whole world; just say it loud enough for the horse's ears to flick back in your direction.

8. **Pet your horse,** but DON'T smack him! Somewhere along the line, people thought smacking a horse was a good thing, and would be interpreted as such by the horse - it must be, since the horse is so big and strong, right? Well, now we know that the horse's skin is even more sensitive than human skin. It stands to reason that a smack feels like a smack, and a pat or rub is a much more appreciated method.

7. Better yet, **slightly release your inside rein while you pet your horse** with your inside hand, in

rhythm with the stride. Can you rub your belly and chew gum at the same time? Then this one is for you!

While your horse is in motion, reach down lightly (but don't lean too far forward as you will change the horse's balance), and move your hand along the horse's neck in a forward/back movement, preferably in rhythm with the horse's head bob. Keep holding the same rein length through the petting action. In canter, this will release the inside rein while the neck is reaching forward/down, and then the contact will be gently taken up again by the time the neck comes back/up again.

The idea is not to interfere with the horse's movement, but to give a gentle inside rein release *while* petting the horse.

6. **Gently (very small movements) open and close your elbows in synch with the horse's body movements** - blend in with him so that he has freedom to swing his head and neck into the movement. You can give through both your elbows in order to move the hands and bit along with the horse. This will create a moment of harmony - no restriction, no instruction, no comment. Just follow along and encourage the horse to take a bolder forward stride thanks to less "stop" from the bit.

5. **Move a little bigger** into the movement of the horse. You always have the option of "releasing" with your seat: let your lower back become loose and supple and follow along in an encouraging, enthusiastic manner - your horse will love the freedom in his back and just might reach further underneath himself with the hind legs in response.

4. *Hold your rein length* but **give a gentle half halt with an ending forward release** so your horse can stretch forward into the contact. In this manner, you can create a small space ahead of the horse that he can reach toward. If done diplomatically, a horse always appreciates feeling the slight freedom of extra space to move forward into.

3. **Stop asking for anything.** Sometimes, it is good enough to stop everything and just let the horse go along for a few strides. Beware - "stopping" doesn't mean that you suddenly drop everything and become a lumpy bumpy bag of jelly that causes the horse to fall to his knees! You can "stop" while maintaining the status quo - keep doing what you

were doing, hold yourself strong and fluid, but just refrain from asking for anything *more* for the time being.

2. **Accept his idea.** Often, a horse will take initiative and offer something that you didn't ask for. Instead of correcting or changing what he did, enjoy the "freebie" and just ride along for a moment. You can get back to your topic in a few strides, but teaching the horse to take initiative, especially in the early stages or when the horse is young, can go far to developing a great rider/horse rapport in the long run.

1. **Do your horse's favorite movement.** All horses have preferred movements that get them all excited! For example, my gelding loves the stretchy trot or canter - he snorts and reaches and the ears flick forward. My mare gets jazzed up with the flying change - again, rambunctious snorts, perky ears, and expression in her face and overall body outline. Find out what your horse's favorite movement is, and then do it at the end of a session or after something difficult!

***

The sooner you can reinforce your horse's actions, the sooner he will connect the reward to the desired behavior. Be light, quick and to the point. Then, go onto the next part of your ride. Look for more to celebrate as you transition into the next movement.

Most importantly, **reward quickly and often.**

9. When Good Riding Instruction Becomes Great

Some people say that a coach can do only so much.

The argument goes like this: after a certain point, there is only so much a riding instructor can say to change a rider's skills. Most of the results come from the rider. After all - if the rider chooses not to (or simply cannot) do what the instructor says, then how much can one person do?

Although it is true that most riders go through difficult learning moments at some point in their riding career, and they might be faced with frustration in a different way than in other sports simply due to the nature of riding a horse, it cannot be said that across the board, riders don't want to put in the effort it takes to improve.

Most of us are riding because of our lifelong passion for horses. Most of us want to serve our horses by being the best rider we can be. Most of us are internally motivated in the first place just because we want to do well and love the feeling of good movement. Most of us want to do the right thing.

Assuming that the rider is in fact *interested* in performing well, how much can an instructor really do to help a rider improve?

When Good Instruction Becomes Great

Great instructors repeatedly show characteristics that make positive effects on their students. They are the ones that make a difference in their riders in one single ride. They are able to send the student home with concrete feedback that can then be used to continue developing independently. What are these traits?

1. Great instruction begins at the student's level.

Great instructors quickly recog-nize the rider's skill level; then, they meet the student with instruction that works to that level. If the student is more of a beginner, the skills being taught might be simplified so that the rider doesn't become too overwhelmed and can achieve success.

The instructor might focus on one or two main points that need to be developed during that ride. For more advanced students, the instructor may come across as more demanding, more particular, more exacting. In each case (and all those in-between), the instructor assumes a different teaching approach that meets the student's needs.

2. Great instructors can explain the basics of the basics exceptionally well.

There is nothing more difficult than trying to explain the most fundamental skills to a rider. The experience of the rider is irrelevant - if there is something that needs to be addressed, then there is no point in going onwards until the basics are addressed. The learning might be the rider's or the horse's - and great instructors will know what to do in each case. Even the most advanced movements are rooted in the basics.

3. Great instructors have an excellent command of the language.

Communication is key, especially for someone who must stand in the middle (or at the side) of a ring while the student is in perpetual motion. The great instructor can change the rider's behavior with only words - well, ok - maybe in conjunction with sounds, energy, gestures and weight shifts to the left and right! But there can be no replacement for a varied and rich vocabulary that can effectively pass on feels and ideas.

4. Great instructors have relevant personal experience.

"There's a difference between knowing the path and walking the path," Morpheus explained to Neo in The Matrix. The truth to that statement cannot be overestimated especially when the instructor is trying to teach something new to a rider. Having a good feeling of what the rider is going through can make the great instructor relate to the stumbling blocks and find a way around them.

5. Great instructors are great problem-solvers.

Many top level trainers speak of the tools we need to collect on our mental toolboxes to solve problems. But toolboxes are not critical to just riders - great instructors have superior problem-solving tools that they have used in different conditions with different riders. Experience is key - not from just a riding perspective, but from a teaching point of view as well.

6. Great instructors help the student set goals but know when to break them.

There is a certain amount of flexibility involved

in great instruction. Although both instructor and rider should be in perpetual evaluation mode, setting new goals and changing them as they are met, the biggest key to meeting goals is the willingness to break from the beaten path when the necessity arises.

Despite having a plan for the day, if during the ride, a completely off-topic situation arises, the great instructor will meet that event head-on without any pre-planning.

7. Great instructors are willing to wait.

They are patient - not only with the rider, but also with the horse. Additionally, they teach their students how to have the same patience when it comes to training the horse.

8. Great instructors are ethical.

They maintain the highest standards of care and welfare for the horse and they teach their students to do the same.

8. Ten Tips For the Average Rider

Are you an average rider? You know the type - the one who has to work hard for one step forward and two steps back. Are you the one who has to spend hours and hours finding your seat, or coordinating your hands and legs to *finally* not interfere with your horse?

Then join the club!

We are the ones who drool wistfully at those riders that seem to just get on the horse and blend into the movement without nary a thought.

We are the ones who need lessons broken down into small, achievable steps that eventually develop into just one coordinated movement. We practice, practice and then practice some more, even while seeming to make only minimal progress.

If you resemble the above scenarios, don't despair. And enjoy the following tips to get through those average rider moments that we all experience from time to time.

1. Find a good teacher.

I use the word "teacher" because the skill development required at the basic levels requires someone that can impart knowledge as well as technique. A good instructor can break down the physiology of movement.

The best instructors can direct you to find feels for yourself. Detailed explanations and clarity of purpose can make the learning curve much easier and even quicker for us average riders.

2. Be patient.

Cut yourself some slack. Then cut your horse some slack. Always seek correct posture, aids, and movements but do it with a sense of humility and gratefulness. Never forget that your horse is working for you and choosing to humor your requests! If something goes wrong, problem solve and patiently redirect your horse's behavior.

3. Practice.

As much as we would like short-cuts, secret methods or fancy expensive gimmicks that will open the world of riding to us, there is no other way to truly become an effective, compassionate rider than to practice. And so we must.

4. Accept your limitations.

Some of us not-as-young riders discover that no matter how hard we try, some parts of our bodies simply never seem to respond the way we would hope!

For example, ligaments and tendons become shortened over time and less resilient. Lower legs have more trouble staying still, or releasing our lower backs to follow the horse becomes more of a challenge. We need to acknowledge that developing more flexible bodies will take longer and harder work. We might need to seek other avenues of physical development such as yoga or Pilates to find that release we are looking for.

5. Find your comfortable un-comfort.

Despite knowing our challenges, we need to constantly seek improvement. Beware of becoming the rider who never develops their skills year after year. Always push yourself past your comfort zone and know that confusion and frustration are part of the learning process. Difficult rides are a good sign that you are going to make a breakthrough (sooner or later)!

6. Enjoy the moment.

Even when we struggle, and certainly during our grandest rides, we must enjoy the moments we get to share with our equine friends. For it is the moment that is what we are here for.

7. Persevere.

Sometimes, it might feel like you are never going to make that breakthrough that you've been looking for. The key at this juncture is to be so determined and stubborn that you will be willing to come back and try again tomorrow and the next day and the day after that.

8. Set goals.

Set long term goals, then develop realistically achievable short-term goals. Be flexible but have an intended path. Even if you don't meet your goals, they will serve to direct your efforts and give you perspective.

9. Read, watch, imitate.

Look out for inspiration. Read the books of the masters as well as contemporary riders. In this day and age of the Internet, having access to excellent video footage of lessons, clinic rides, and show footage is at your fingertips.

Watch many riders, define what you like in a good ride and study. Then, go and try it yourself. Imitation is the first step to learning a skill set. Watch and try. Get feedback from your instructor. Once you have developed a skill, you can easily make the skill "yours" by adding something new or specific to your horse's needs.

10. Keep practicing.

Develop a routine. Follow a pre-determined path. Keep at it. There is no other way.

7. Why You Don't Need To Force Your Heels Down In Horseback Riding

Everywhere we go, people focus on the one position fault that is easiest to identify: the heels. In general, it is perfectly obvious if the heels are up, level or down.

I know that everyone has always told you to get your heels lower. You've probably been told that you have to drop your heels so that you can have better balance and contact with your horse's side. They've said that the longer leg stabilizes your balance and gives better aids.

All over the Internet, people give good advice: "Try to get your heels lower. Then your position will be perfect."

So we grin and bear it. Despite the discomfort, we push those heels down. We grunt and groan while we try to keep the heel down through the transitions, bends, and canters. We do what we gotta do to make it look good.

Why We Shouldn't Force the Heels Down

Some of us have an easy time getting the heels down. If you are one of those people, you will wonder why the rest of us have to work so hard at it. For other people, overall body tightness plays a factor in how they can release through the legs.

When you push down, you drive tension into your leg. Invariably, the tightness in the heels cause the knees to pinch on the saddle. The knees cause tightness in the thighs and then you find your seat has an uncontrollable tendency to bounce against the horse's movement.

Aside from the effects on your body and position, you also affect the horse. The tight knees prevent the horse from moving freely and might contribute to sluggishness in the horse's movement, reluctance to swing through the back and in the long term, even gait abnormalities.

There is no way to force your heel down without causing some sort of unwanted result. The tension in your heels can transfer all the way up the leg and into your seat.

What To Do Instead

In order to get your heels down the way we see in the equitation books or by more advanced riders, you need to develop suppleness through your joints and tendons. This requires a long-term commitment to changing the way your body moves. You simply cannot force the joints and tendons to position themselves in a way that helps both you and your horse without either having natural softness in your legs, or by developing it over time off the horse's back.

There are several ways to train suppleness into your leg. Many activities can help - dancing, gymnastics, yoga - anything that helps to stretch and loosen and strengthen especially the legs.

If you are not the type to cross-train, you can work on the same thing by standing on the edge of a staircase. Hang your heel off the edge of the stair and let it lengthen so that it drops below your toes. Then stay there for a minute or so, just letting the joints and tendons learn to release in that position.

Once you are on the horse, the key is that the *whole* leg has to stretch - right from the hips. The hips release, the knees soften and the calves sit even closer to the horse's side. Only then will the heels stretch below the toes - all on their own. It's not good enough to just push those heels down.

When you first get the "real" stretch, it feels incredible. The leg really truly becomes long and you feel like you've wrapped your legs right around the horse in a wonderful bear-hug. The hips open enough to let the legs dangle down so that the legs and seat seem to just flow effortlessly along with the horse's movements. There is less struggle to stay with the horse because you supple *into* the horse. The best part is that your ankles just naturally "drop"- in the sense that they couldn't possibly be anywhere other than below your toes.

There is no force, no push, no positioning. It just is.

In the Meantime...

Riding more frequently will definitely help. But remember one thing: don't force the heels.

If you ride with level heels, then ride with level heels. Although you shouldn't ride with lifted heels, be aware of the opposite extreme: the forced heels. If you do push your heels down, be cognizant of the effects on your seat. If you notice your seat perching in the saddle, or your knees pinching on the saddle, lighten up the pressure on your heels.

Know that correctly dropped heels are a product of suppleness and length in the leg. Work on changing your body, not on just the appearance of your position.

6. How to Halt Without Pulling On The Reins

Does your horse get offended when you pull on the reins to stop? Does he pin his ears, shake his head, hollow his back and *keep going*?

Maybe he's trying to tell you something: stop

pulling on the reins!

There is a way to get your horse to stop without pulling on the reins.

But first, you both have to be "in sync" together, working in tandem instead of against each other.

If you haven't done this before, it may take a few tries to convince your horse that you want to work with him. Horses that are regularly pulled on seem to accept that the pressure has to be there before they should respond. They might learn to lean on the bit, pulling against you while you pull backward, hoping for the legs to stop.

Some horses are generous and eventually slow their feet, stop/starting until finally, all four legs come to a halt. Other horses might not be quite as forgiving and just keep going until you have to put more and more pressure on the mouth. Eventually, one of you wins but it's never pretty!

We all dream of finding the halt that looks like we are in complete harmony with our horse. You know - the one that feels like the horse's legs are your legs, and your mind is so coordinated with the horse that it looks like you are reading each other's thoughts.

It does happen. The secret: ride from your seat. I'm perfectly aware of the fact that we've talked about the seat many times already, but there is no other answer. Everything in horseback riding begins and ends with the seat.

The instructions below might sound quite complicated. Initially, developing the timing and coordination of aids should be! Learning correct aids should be a lifelong quest for most of us, and if we have old, ingrained habits (like pulling on the reins), these changes may take even longer.

But in the long run, you won't have to think anything through and the aids will happen together on their own.

Setup for a Correct Halt

1. Contact

Prepare several strides ahead of the intended location. Your reins should be a good length - not too long and not too short. There should be a steady enough contact on the bit to be able to communicate very subtle changes of pressure.

2. Begin a series of half-halts.

The half-halts start at the seat. In rhythm with the horse's movement, resist with your lower back. Be sure to resist in rhythm. In other words, your lower back and seat will feel something like this: *resist... flow... resist... flow... resist... flow.*

2a. Use your legs.

During each *flow* moment, squeeze lightly with your lower legs. This helps the horse engage his hind end deeper underneath the body in preparation with the halt.

2b. Use the hands.

During each *resist* moment, squeeze the reins with your hands. You might squeeze both reins or just one rein (the outside rein being the usual rein) but in any case, do your best to use the hands after the leg aids. The rein pressure should occur in tandem with the resisting seat aid.

3. When you are ready for the halt, simply stop your seat.

Maintain contact with your legs and reins, but stop the activity. *Don't keep pulling on the reins.* If the horse is truly with you, his legs will stop lightly and in balance.

***

Horses that have been trained to respond to the half-halt will sigh in relief when you lighten up on your aids and use your seat in the halt. You might be surprised at how easily the legs will stop if you can improve your timing and releases.

Horses that have always been pulled on might not respond at all. They might be expecting to be hauled backward, thrown to the forehand, and dragged to a stop. If this is the case, be patient. If you haven't done this before, it may take a few tries to convince your horse that you want to work with him.

You might have to bridge the learning gap by applying the half-halts several times, stopping your seat and then pulling to stop. In the end though, the pull should disappear completely from your vocabulary (exception: in an emergency stop).

Regardless of how you get there, the goal is to stop all four legs in a light, balanced manner that allows the horse to use his hind end when he takes that last step. Your horse might walk a few strides and then halt.

If you feel your horse's front end lighten into the halt, you know you are on the right track. If you discover the four legs stopped square and parallel to each other, pet and gush over him, and call it a day!

5. Here' How (And Why) You Should Ride With Bent Elbows

Have you ever watched riders going around the ring with straight, stiff arms?

What have you noticed?

The exact opposite of what they probably want is happening. Although they are likely trying to be quiet and still, their hands are in fact bouncing up and down with the horse's movement. The end result is an on-again, off-again contact with the horse's mouth - in other words, a pull/release repeated over and over.

Some horses truck along and find ways to hide behind the pressure, and other horses complain through head shaking, rooting of the reins, or shortening their strides till the movement minimizes. In every case, the communication between horse and rider suffers.

Of course, we know very well that contact

is more than just about the hands and reins. But for today's purpose, we'll focus on one part of the body: the elbows.

1. Hang Your Upper Arm Straight Down

The ideal arm position is one that keeps a vertically straight upper arm. Essentially, the upper arm belongs to your body. In other words, if the upper arm comes off the body either forward *or* backward, the arm is interfering with the horse in some way.

The arms (and hands) should only aid in conjunction with the seat and upper body aids anyway. Therefore, keeping the upper arm on the body helps to prevent what we would naturally like to do - move the arm forward and backward in attempt to influence our horse.

2. Create A Light "L" Shape in Your Elbows

While your upper arm stays on the body, your lower arm comes off the body toward the horse's mouth. The arm takes the shape of a soft "L", hands staying in line with the reins that go to the horse's mouth.

Elbows cannot point out ("chicken elbows") nor pull backward (pulling).

In this way, your arms will position your hands quite naturally a couple of inches in front of the saddle pommel. That is the ideal place for the hands.

3. Put Some Life Into the Elbows and Wrists

Now all you need is to find lightness in the joints. It is almost counter intuitive that stillness comes from movement (but it does make sense if you think about it). At first, it might feel awkward while you try to figure out how to move your elbows so that your hands can stay still on the reins.

Try This Trick

Hold your reins with your hands in front of the pommel with the light "L" shape in your elbows. Get the horse moving (walk, trot or canter). Put your pinkies down on the front of the saddle pad and work out how you must move your elbows to keep the hands steady on the pad. Once your hands are fairly steady, lift them off the pad and keep the elbows active in the same way.

After you have discovered soft, moving joints in your arms (all the way from the shoulder down), you will wonder how you ever could go with straight or pulling arms. You will discover so many benefits.

Your horse might move forward more eagerly, start to swing through the back and maybe even give you a snort or two. All your aids will "go through" softly and with less interference, making communication suddenly easy and matter-of-fact.

But the bottom line is that your horse will benefit from a kinder, gentler bit that communicates rather than punishes. And isn't this what we are always aiming for?

4. 9 Things You Need To Know If You Want To Ride Horses

You might have liked horses all your life.

Or you might have had an awakening not too long ago that is urging you to explore horseback riding for the first time.

You can't tear your eyes away from the sight of glowing coats and rippling muscles.

You get excited every time you drive by horses in a field.

Contrary to your friends, you even like the smell of a barn!

And now, you know you are ready to take the first steps on the long road of becoming an equestrian. You've booked riding lessons at a local barn and you are convinced that you are ready to tackle the learning curve that lays ahead. Before you begin, here are nine tips to smooth the way into your new adventures!

1. Be prepared to be a beginner - for a long time!

Once you step into that stirrup for the first time, forget all about instant gratification. Instead, get all pumped up for the accomplishment of doing something for the long term.

Don't worry if your fingers fumble when putting on the bridle. Have no worry when the horse gives you a knowing look out of the corner of his eye: "This one is a beginner!" Just take the plunge into new feels, new learning curves and new coordination. It's all about the joys (and challenges) of being on the path.

2. Every horse has something to teach you.

If you ride at a riding school, and have had the chance to ride many horses over the course of a few years, you will truly understand that there is something to be learned from every horse you ride.

If you part-board or lease a horse, you can have the opportunity to work with one horse over the long term. You might develop a deeper relationship and maybe even know each other so well that you can read each other's minds. But always be appreciative of the chance to ride new horses because they will add to your depth of experience and repertoire of "language" you need to ride effectively.

3. Find an excellent mentor.

Your mentor might or might not be your instructor. However, this person will be critical to the success of your first years as a horse rider. She will be the one who can listen to your questions and concerns and give you the answers you need for your situation. She will guide you in your decisions and help you find the solutions that are necessary for your development - even if you are not aware of them at the time. Find someone you can trust.

4. Surround yourself with great professionals and horse friends.

It is true that you are the sum of the influences around you. So search for people you admire and look up to. Find the ones who you would like to emulate. Then, be around them and learn from them at every opportunity.

Get to know the professionals in your area - from nutrition, to health care, to training - it is essential for you to be surrounded by kind, compassionate people who always put the horse first when they make decisions.

5. Although the initial learning seems quick and easy, don't despair once your learning curve seems to slow down.

At some point, your riding skills will plateau and try as you might, new learning becomes frustrating and difficult. Be ready for that time period and be willing to keep trudging through - until you reach your next series of leaps and bounds. However, the plateaus will always reappear just before the next real learning curve; they are just a fact of life.

6. Be ready to be physical in a way you've never experienced before.

Riding is like no other sport because of the presence of the horse.

Rubbing your belly and chewing gum is an easy task compared to riding! In order to truly move with the horse, you have to learn to coordinate body parts you never knew you had, and then *also* stay on top of a moving 1,000 pound animal! But have no fear - it will all come together in the long run.

7. Watch, read, study, do.

It goes without saying that there is much learning to be done off the horse's back. Read books to study what the movements should be like. Watch videos of professionals and even amateurs (especially now that videos are so easily accessible on the Internet). Go to clinics and watch how other riders develop under the eye of an experienced clinician. Then take your own lessons, ride at clinics and shows or video yourself. Use every available means to solicit feedback.
Then study some more!

8. Be wary of the "a little knowledge is a dangerous thing" stage.

This happens to everyone at least once in their riding career. There eventually comes a time, once you have made your mistakes and learned from them, that you begin to feel pretty confident about your equine-related skills. The tack no longer defies you. You develop the balance and coordination needed to walk, trot and canter without feeling like you might fall off any second. You can even ride and talk at the same time!

When it all starts to come together like this, you might become a little more confident than were at the beginning. You start to take more riding risks. You might think about changing routines to suit yourself better - change the barn, or ditch your instructor!

Before you head off into the land of grass is greener everywhere else, heed these words! You will want to spread your wings and fly - that is a fact.

However, although there are certainly many ways to Rome, especially in the equine world, don't "instructor hop". Nothing is more confusing than trying to comprehend different people's systems over and over again.

9. Listen to your horse.

Although it sounds a little far-fetched, it is indeed possible to "hear" your horse if you understand their routines, structures and communications. If life is good, your horse will show you his pleasure by becoming more rideable. He will be calm but at the same time responsive to you. He will improve his ground manners, develop consistency under saddle, and work with you toward a better partnership.

If, on the other hand, he becomes less receptive, more difficult to handle, and lose overall condition, you will know this is not the path you want to be on. Just listen and then make decisions according to the feedback.

Well, there you have it! Hopefully, these tips will help you as you progress from newbie to old-timer!

3. The #1 Rider Problem: The Outside Rein!

Among all of our riding challenges, this problem is the one that should be on the top of the list.

The outside rein is the most underused and poorly understood of all the aids, and here's why. Human beings, as bi-peds, are hand-fixated.

That is, we do *everything* with our hands. Being vertically inclined, we lean forward and almost in all interactions, reach toward something with our hands. It stands to reason that we should use this same mechanism when it comes to riding. For example, steering a horse is as simple as steering a bike - just grab the rein on the turn side and pull! The horse's head turns in that direction, and the legs must follow.

Right?

WRONG!!

One of the most incomprehensible things that we humans have to deal with when we decide to ride horses, is to reprogram our natural tendency to lean forward and pull on the rein. It is a most unfortunate undertaking, as this natural inclination is so hardwired in us that it feels wrong to stay balanced on top of a moving horse and use our leg and seat aids before our hands. And so we start on a long journey of "re-wiring"...

... and one of the most difficult concepts in riding happens to be the use of the outside rein. We become experts at riding with a tight inside rein and a loopy outside rein. We teach the horse to stiffen on the inside jaw and "pop" the outside shoulder. We ride up the rail with the shoulder "out" and the haunches "in" - almost moving diagonally without knowing it. If we only knew how simple it would be to allow the horse to move straight - using a straightening outside rein!

What to do?

The solution to the outside rein lies in the inside leg and seat bone. You've heard it time and again: "inside leg to outside rein". Well, it's not *really* about your leg - it's about the horse's balance. The horse needs to "step away" from your leg in order to take his weight more to the outside. This will help him stretch the outside of his body, bend toward the inside and "fill" your outside rein.

Your inside seat bone encourages the weight shift. It accepts the thrust of the inside hind leg and then shifts the weight even more to the outside. In this way, you help your horse balance as you go around the ring. And somehow miraculously, you discover you have an outside rein!

Now, it is your responsibility to maintain this new connection. That is, use the "contact" - don't abuse it by throwing it away! Give when needed, take when needed, resist when necessary (or preferably, do all three in a split second!). But by all means, *keep it connected!* If you can keep the rein straight, you will also keep your horse straight - through the shoulders and neck (your legs are responsible for the horse's hips).

So on your next ride, remember the outside rein. But remember even more, that it's not just about grabbing the rein - it's about setting the horse up through its body so that he "fills" the outside rein. Then, *when you have one, do something with it!*

Of course, this is just the tip of the iceberg. This is just the "irritating" thought - the one that sparks you on to delving deeper into the subject. We all know that finding that outside rein (correctly) is no easy feat. The best path to this solution is to find a competent instructor who can give you consistent, accurate feedback. Good luck and happy riding.

2. Why You Don't Want To Pull On The Inside Rein (And What To Do Instead)

When we ride horses, we often assume that the inside rein is used like the steering wheel of a car or a bicycle. We think that by pulling on the horse from the inside, the horse must obviously turn his nose and then follow it. Right?

Pulling to Turn

In some cases, the turn does happen. The horse's body moves along the direction of the head and he accommodates us the best he can. This is the reason why many of us think we are on the right track by pulling to turn.

However, at some point in time, we begin to better understand the biomechanics of pulling and how it affects the horse's body.

Sometimes, although the horse turns his nose in the direction of the pull, his body continues in the original trajectory. He doesn't easily make the turn. Other times, his body even goes in the *opposite direction* (in effect, drifting out) from where we pointed his nose! Has this ever happened to you?

Then we learn about the usefulness of the outside rein in turns. We practice using the outside rein while turning until it eventually becomes a habit.

But there is one other consequence to pulling on that inside rein that has little to do with turning. It isn't as straightforward to identify or visualize. And it affects the horse under almost every circumstance - on a turn, over a straight line, in a gait change, through a half-halt and more.

Blocking the Inside Hind Leg

If you want to prevent the inside hind leg from coming through underneath the body, this is how you do it: *pull back on the inside rein.*

The only problem is that the haunches cannot support the horse's balance.

Without the hind end as the engine, the horse is left to having to initiate movement from his front legs. He must then drag his body (and yours) along from the front, thus losing balance and falling to the forehand. You know the rest: tripping, stumbling, tension, rock-hard hollow back, discomfort and so on.

What NOT To Do

Most people's reaction is to do the exact opposite and fully drop the inside rein. Sometimes, you can even see the droop as if the rider wants to say, "See? I don't even have any contact at all!"

Having absolutely no contact can be counterproductive too, because then there is no way for you to support the horse when necessary. You will end up with an on-again, off-again pull that becomes difficult for the horse to negotiate. In the end, no contact can be as bad as too much contact.

There is always a happy medium.

What To Do

You have three strategies.

#1 is the easiest to do while #3 takes the most coordination. You can probably progress through the steps as you become better able to find that release. Your horse might also have a preference between the three at different times - so you can use the skill that suits him best in the moment.

Please note: these techniques can be used in the same manner on a snaffle bit (short rein length) or any curb/shank bit (long rein length) or anything in-between! Please feel free to try this in your riding style and discipline.

1. You could let out an inch of rein.

Lengthening the rein an inch out might be all the horse needs to encourage freedom in the hind quarters. The rein is therefore short enough for us to communicate with him at a moment's notice, but long enough that there is that space for him to reach - from his hind legs, over his topline and through the poll to the bit.

There is no better feeling than when the horse *reaches* for the bit into the rein space you just gave him!

2. You could maintain the same rein length and let out your elbow.

This strategy gives the horse the same feeling as #1 but you don't need to let out the rein length.

When is it useful to maintain the same rein length?

When you know you need to be able to give clear and timely half-halts in order to help the horse maintain balance through a variety of movements. For example, if your instructor is asking you to negotiate several movements in sequence, you won't have the time to let the rein out and take it back, and doing so will unnecessarily disrupt your horse's balance.

Instead, you just let your elbows out and take them back in the following strides. The effect is the same - the horse gets a release and then a take-up for further communication.

3. You could move better with the horse with the same rein and contact pressure.

This one is the icing on the cake.

If you can move through your *entire body*, staying in sync with the horse's movements but releasing where and when needed, you will have one happy, confident, bold moving horse. You might need to release through your seat. You might "loosen" through the inside shoulder, allowing the inside hind to reach within a moment's notice. Maybe your legs need to "breathe" with your horse's sides.

In any case, riding in tandem with the horse is something we always aspire to and there is good reason for that. When you both move "as one", the earth stops rotating and you float on that ninth cloud!

Letting the inside hind leg do its job is one of the first keys to riding with the horse in mind.

1. Ten Habits Of Competent Riders

We can all think of a rider we know that seems to always do well, has calm, happy horses, and steadily improves their horse's physical and mental state in an almost effortless manner.

We watch and admire from afar, but in fact, we can all stand to learn from their regular habits and "way of being" in order to develop our own horse riding mantra.

What do great riders have in common that makes them appealing to watch, steadily develop their riding skills and become role models for others to aspire to emulate?

1. Persistence: Great riders are willing to try, try again. They know that there will be more rides, more days, and the slow and steady approach always wins the "race".

2. Open-mindedness: Great riders know there is something to be learned from everyone, even if to see proof of why NOT to do something. These riders are not discipline exclusive, and are always aware that good riding is good riding is good riding, regardless of the saddle or style.

3. Patience: Great riders are willing to wait to reap the rewards. They know that even if something falls apart today, there will be more days to come and small steps even backward are more beneficial than quick fixes or shortcuts.

4. Quitting: This may seem counter-intuitive, but great riders quit while they're ahead. They ride for short periods of time to their highest ability and then call it a day. They seem to intuitively know when enough is enough.

5. Effectiveness: Great riders seek maximum effectiveness with minimum harm. They make every step count, and they resist overriding the horse for the sake of performance.

6. Self-Improvement: Great riders regularly seek to upgrade their riding skills and general horse education. They are willing to spend time, money and humility in the quest for constant self-improvement.

7. Seeing the Big Picture: Great riders enjoy the "work" and the path as much as they do the goal achievement. They know that each day and each step is as important as the other and is a natural progression in development.

8. Role Models: Great riders know great riding when

they see it and seek to surround themselves with those who will not only help them improve on a riding level, but also on a more personal and inspirational level as well.

9. Problem Solving: Great riders can trouble-shoot through problems to come to gratifying solutions. They have many tools in their "tool-boxes" and know there is more than one way to approach a situation. They are always willing to try new things.

10: Horse Listeners: Good riders are expert horse listeners! They are sensitive to the feedback from their horses and adjust their responses accordingly.

It's as simple as that!

Other Books By The Author

Horse Listening – The Book: Stepping Forward To Effective Riding

The first book of the Horse Listening Collection. A compilation of chapters focused specifically on the rider. Digital download.

Horse Listening – Book 2: Forward and Round To Training Success

In this second book, chapters focus on riding and training to improve your horse's quality of movement.

Horse Listening – Book 3: Horses. Riding. Life

The third and final book of the collection. Read about how horses and riding impact our lives.

Goal Setting For The Equestrian: A Personal Workbook

A different kind of workbook to help you keep track of your riding goals. Designed specifically for the equestrian. Write into the pages, print off as many copies as you need.

ABOUT THE AUTHOR

Kathy Farrokhzad is an Equestrian Canada certified riding instructor of over 20 years. She has been personally trained, ridden and shown in several riding disciplines including western performance, natural horsemanship, long distance competitive trail (endurance) and most prominently, dressage. She is a Dressage Canada Bronze Medal recipient and has bred, raised and trained her own young horses to the show ring.

She is author of the *Horse Listening Collection* and *Goal Setting For the Equestrian: A Personal Workbook.*